MW01317026

KYLE J. KNAPP

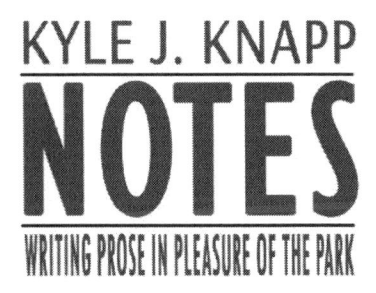

NOTES
WRITING PROSE IN PLEASURE OF THE PARK

Copyright © 2017 by Meta L. Knapp

All Rights Reserved. No part of this book may be reproduced in any form or by any means without the prior written consent of the publisher, except where permitted by law.

Memorial tributes by Kayla Knapp and Aaron Warner used with permission.

Excerpt of "The Philosophy of Sailing" used with permission. Copyright © by Justin Frederick.

"Twin Talk" © 2014 by Patti Abbott, first published in *The Lizard's Ardent Uniform*, Volume I of the Veridical Dreams series.

Special thanks to Amanda Shaw for the inclusion of "As I See More Glass."

Cover and interior artwork by Kyle J. Knapp. Back cover photograph of Kyle's notebooks taken by Kayla Knapp. Cover design by dMix. Author photograph by Eustina Daniluk.

ISBN: 978-1-943035-26-7

www.beattoapulp.com

Contents

A Sister's Eulogy *by Kayla Knapp* i

Caroline 1

Cerement 2

Oh, Rural Joys 3

Red Arctic Air-Raids 4

An Envelope of Evergreen 5

Dear Somnus 6

Writing Prose in Pleasure of the Park 8

A Mansion in the Moor 12

The Man with Four Shadows 13

The King of Ithaca 14

Sunrise on Saturn 16

The Sixth Season 17

To Live to be Alone 18

The Lonely Hour 20

This Life We Won't Remember 22

Notes 23

Women in Acrostics 27

Seawall of City Lights 28

Enantiomers and Techgrind Lyrics 29

However Does the Ocean Circle the Ion Sphere 30

The Neighbor 32

June 38

Raspberry Ashes Splashed 39

The Amazing Lives We Wait 40

In a Shed under Water 41

As I See More Glass *with Amanda Shaw* 43

The Favonian Eclipse 50

Pamela Susan, Cloy with Grief 52

The Morning of Pamona and Vertumnus 53

Somniferum 54

For Ava 55

Everyone in the World 57

An Interview with the Author 59

A Friend's Eulogy *by Aaron Warner* 63

About the Author 67

BONUS STORY: Twin Talk *by Patti Abbott* 71

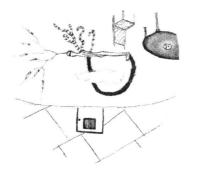

From the poetry collection of Kyle J. Knapp
PLUVIAL GARDENS

PHRYGIA

Warm crying dream
Of women damp in evening clouds
"Phrygia; Land of Roses"
Where Aeolus is king
That is where they took her
On a paper ship.

Take a walk through the *Pluvial Gardens*, a debut collection of twenty-four poems where nature is explored in tandem with the darker side of relationships, life, and death.

From the poetry collection of Kyle J. Knapp
CELEBRATIONS IN THE OSSUARY

THE PERFECT DAY

Give me just a day
    Of homemade wine,
Spray-painted sunflowers,
19th century prose,
Sordid, puerile jokes,
Dried maple leaves to crush
    in our palms
A pale too-old sun to dance
    beyond

    And her laughter—

Celebrations in the Ossuary is a dark, unflinching ride into the core of a young man, on a poetic journey to uncover the inner truth about himself and the world around him.

A Sister's Eulogy

I cannot begin to share with you all the countless memories I have of my brother Kyle. When we were young, I envied my brother in all that he did. Wherever Kyle was, it was certain that a young, blonde-haired girl wasn't far behind.

I have never known another person as loving as my brother. Everything that Kyle did, he did with a full and open heart. My brother didn't see the world as many of us do. Kyle saw the beauty in the simple aspects of life. Kyle never did what was expected. It wasn't important to him to be the best, or the most successful, it was only important for Kyle to be Kyle. I felt so safe in his surrounding, and so blessed by his presence.

Over the past few days, I've looked at myself each morning, and I have seen Kyle within me. He taught me so much about how to love without judgment, how to be myself even when faced with persuasion, and how to capture the magic of laughter.

Kyle had always promised me that his writing would never become famous until he was gone, but in my eyes, he was always legendary. Most of all, I will miss that captivating smile that my brother possessed. Kyle always wanted to live in a world absent of hate, of restriction and conventionalism, and now my brother is finally free. My love has only grown stronger in the days that I have spent without him, and in all that I do, I hope that I make you proud, big brother.

—Kayla Knapp
June 22, 2013

| NOTES |

Caroline

Caroline
Ice-trellis blue
Of a lost childhood, dolorous
Of nostalgia—
I've come lovelorn

She's Annabel Lee
Metamorphosed
After all these years

She's Ligeia's ghost
Crumbling in her white dress
At the top of the stairs

She's Berenice
Immortalized
For all time—
With me

But really,
She's just Carrie
Young again
With her crazed mother
And her tawny sun-dried skin.

Cerement

The ptarmigan
With broken wing
Bent back, bone white,
Limps through the osier
In the alpine snow
Sepulchered behind the bottle-green glass
Of a handheld globe.

Oh, Rural Joys

In the attic, a slovenly man
with bright amber eyes paces.
Cracked and burnt driftwood floorboards
underneath his sandals.
He shakes torrents of dust from his long, gray beard,
raving madly at the empty bottle
alone on the school desk in the corner.

A lurid cyclorama of gold-frosted costumes,
dusty with lice,
drape the walls
and lift in the cold wind,
dancing to life.

All the windows are open
and then sudden sunlight glares
for which he stops, silently,
acknowledging the morning sun.

The Red Arctic Air-Raids

I want to wake up with gray hair
And blood in my cheeks
Smiling,
Without regret

I want to wake up in a spring flowerbed
That smells like Cognac,
With dragonfly wings drowsed over the lids of my eyes
Dreaming of deserts across the channel

Oh, tomorrow,
Will you help me to write home again?
Will you help me sleep?
Through this red arctic air-raid,
Through another tired season?

An Envelope of Evergreen

An envelope of evergreen
Enshrouded by time
A fainted sea of pale gladiolus
In pale Atlantic fog
Crosses the crown
Of the bracken overgrowth

The broken branch falls into
The antechamber of the summer wold
Through which, you see the world,
the ruin
And the rain outside
the bedroom ball

Dear Somnus

Fingers ledge-lost
He holds out his wrinkled hands
Falling from his window
Bedgown billowing out
Prostrate in an orange silence
—for a long time—
A ripened glow emerges,
And springs forth from his chest

Oh, dear Somnus,
Brightened from sleep and lowered still
To the ocean in woe
With one dream he will never forget

Here lies Somnus
Towers dark and sea-cast
To a hell
—for all time—
Cold to touch
Absent of breath

On his side in clay he lay, dethroned
But a picture pulses in the lifeless black
Of that dream he'll never forget
Of a New York kiss.

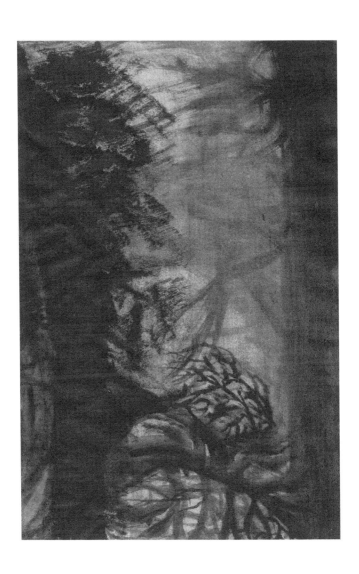

Writing Prose in Pleasure of the Park

I go about my morning routine, eating a two-egg, corned-venison, cheese and tomato omelet for breakfast, with an apple on the side, and then I wash it down with a beer while watching an episode of *Dexter*.

This morning I have circumvented my spent feint in the "Laborman's Lot" by surrendering eight more hours to the impending poverty of eight days of lost pay. But I also have good reason. The weekend before this last, I injured my cervical vertebrae by whiplash and my lumbar by contusion after jumping off Sackett Bridge into the narrow channel that flows into Beebe Lake. I took the leap at an awkward and nefarious angle, just to impress a girl. In all fairness, that chick was hot.

I pick up *Dune* and look at the clock: eleven thirty. And I begin to read …. I look at the clock again: it's now three in the afternoon. Time to pack up four cans of Budweiser and, what the heck, a Kashi granola bar into my bag and I head off to Mill Dam Park where I find a quiet bench on which to journal. As I sit here, I realize that the hard, wooden seat is aggravating to my recent injuries.

Lest my ambitions are effaced by sad disposition, I shouldn't regret to leave this park much sooner than planned. The discomfort along with the damp and dark surroundings, matted in a storm shadow of the snow that will persist for months to come. But with my soul's reflection here—in the tree's sloping shoulders and swaying arms, in the pureness of air floating on eddies delivering wisps of an earthy pungency—it's difficult to depart when paragraphs remain unfinished.

I see yesterday's footprints in the well-trodden ground. My park is being capered by children's play, and elderly visitors calling themselves "amateur ornithologists." Then there are friends who, so very long ago I, myself, had introduced them to the charm of this preserve; who then brought friends, and who brought still others; amassing as a foul ambage of some juggernaut hydra-monster that I can now truly dislike without ever having met a single one of them.

Of course, there's always a foul new generation of adventurous, puerile urchins who deserve these woods, just like we did, to make "squirting noises in the brush"— I think that is a William Burroughs quote … a weird bastard that, to be quite honest, I never understood a word. They always seem to get caught now though, issued to Camp Green Lake. Only heard from, a little later, when The Baby is born too soon to ever grant society its surmise.

I was at first amazed by the general naïve innocence of my father's time, and the liberty of his childhood life. But now, it seems like even my own generation, as painfully outlandish as most of our "rules" were, caught us a break somewhere in time; at a time in history that has now become oddly nostalgia, forevermore.

Sallow leafless-listless-lifeless branch
Remind me why I choose not to leave
Before I empty every bottle?
Why am I so saddened by every man's story?
By every man's failed dream?

Back to work tomorrow.
A continuing form of bondage
Where I can't drink beer and write prose in the park
Where I can't construct riddles
Or plan revolutions
Or, at the very least, abuse myself in the curtain-dark
Like a hairy, one-armed hunchback—left hand mind
you.

Morrison once said,
"We need to find an answer instead of a way,"
But now, we truly can't
"Resolve the past,"
We truly cannot
Live again,
Even by the quiet quay where I wander and wonder
And drift away.

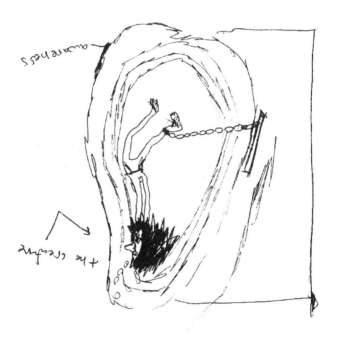

The Mansion in the Moor

Tinseled towers boast
Of a chandelier that bursts
Into a thousand painted swallows
That all die captive before the window, gray, cold.

There are chairs that stack themselves
Into pantomime pieces
Lamps that flounce, crash, and then take another form
Ancient lemures that jump the spire
Mahogany floors that burst into flame
Pianos that all by themselves play and play and play!

A wreath that grows roots
That rot to the ground
A dog with nine lives, that barks like a man
And a blood-splattered wall
That blinks in the wonderful bright colors of Christmas.

Each season the mansion crumbles
And rebuilds itself in another form
Somewhere down the river
On a path beyond the moor.

The Man with Four Shadows

The Man with Four Shadows
Stepped quietly forth from the boardwalk
Bringing terror
And sickness to the village
With his absinthe-green thoughts.

—Death.

In a pale hand outstretched
Lay an ocher-core rose,

Then everyone dyed the colors,
Howling.

The Man with Four Shadows spun round
And without them, he left.

The King of Ithaca

An old man dragged the marsh
Dragged the marina
Dragged under the bridge—

He amassed a mountain of dead drag-queens
    and drug addicts
And dirty, old wine-bottle chimes
And covered it all with baize
    in the center of main street.

Then, the good doctor barked from the
iron-framed window
    With a butterfly net
        Nailed to his hand
"Hale, Hestia! We've uncovered the murder weapon!"
The policemen grabbed each other's asses
And giggled by the fountain
As the body of Minerva
Washed up in the salt mines
Bereft a right shoe.

The Ithacans built pyres
And released concentrated bath-salts clouds
Into the atmosphere
And all at once began to eat their own skin off

Hanging dogs from flagpoles
Pulling live wires out of walls
Free at last to fall over and take it
Just like they've always secretly fought to
All of these years.

Sunrise on Saturn

Porcelain-blue butterflies burst
Into the orient whorl
Below the wharf

Porcelain-blue birds explode
From mountain shadow
Of the snowy wold

A man watering seaweeds
Turns away
When nubile dawn strokes his garden
Like a riverbed blooming
Across the rings of Saturn

The Sixth Season

A crowding of pine trees
Warmly covered
With a film of copper-colored
        Snowfall.
Is this the first thing I saw
When I woke up
4,000 years after the bomb?

I was lying on a frozen pond.
A dog with long, tangled,
Thorn-like hair
Was bleeding to death
On a small island.

I crawled to it on the burnished ice
Only to have it break around me

And from that forsaken isle
I floated away
Into the pearly-orange afterglow
Of the sixth season.

To Live to be Alone

Draughts of snow are killing me
Solitude is killing me
Whiskey is killing me.

The warm summer sun is killing me
The human race is killing everything
Sobriety is driving me insane and off the rails
Weaving through traffic in the lavender light of a
thunderstorm

What more is left to be said?
What more is left to be done

A funeral party betrayed me
An epitaph saw to my final word
        —Wandering down the road
Beyond the expanse alone
(and at last without the noise)

The Lonely Hour

I've been sitting at my desk in the corner, jittery, vertebral column still jarred from an ill-considered exploit, trying to write a poem on a piece of crumpled scrap paper I found in my back pocket. The cup of coffee in front of me has been inimical to my reflexive disorder as well as my creative flow. The poem goes:

> *Virginia, share your pillow*
> *Council your unrest*
> *Your bold, but broken words*
> *Have never far to fall*
> *Virginia, share your 'whettle'*
> *Speak to me of the bleary mountain loom*
> . . . .

But I can't finish it, because I'm just not interested in what I'm writing. I wonder if I may be losing my propensity for letters. I remember a movie with John Travolta playing a hapless, alcoholic literatus who champions the expression: *Get rid of the bottle, get rid of the genie*. Or something like that, and nothing could feel truer at this lonely hour.

This Life We Won't Remember
('The Rape of Proserpine')

By summer
When I walk with her,
By winter
When they'll pull her away,
I always thought I'd love her
For that stolen blush of death in her smile.

But what does it even matter,
Who cares if everyone else dies?

I had always thought I'd wed her
Under Aurora, sick with mourning,
I saw us sitting in the dawn.

But what does it even matter,
In this life we won't remember.

As loving as I'd known her,
The seraphs danced before her,
Before they pulled her down, into the ground
And took her away.

Notes (a poetic rendition based on "The Philosophy of Sailing" by Justin Frederick)

The grayed prison ship
Sinking under starlight
    Crumpled, shrinking—papered and pale

White lightning pulsed,
    Spangling the shoreline
        And silvering the foliage,
            Threatening a rainstorm.

The caves we saw from afar
Were falling to the ocean floor
And past them we three walked
Afraid to look into the hearth

When the boardwalk collapsed
From blood-rusted-through nails,
Our ankles broke.

And into the ocean tile we tumbled
Screaming all,
Falling below the glimmering surface
Of the island tempest

A brilliant midnight lightning-strike
So gilded the shadows
Of our tired, torn-out
Human-born souls,
That we wept in silence
And paced forth and back.

Part 2
Weary men, come stand on stone pillars.
Come now, are we to stand
Naked,
Alone.

"Where are we?"
"Who among us have lost sons tonight?"
"Has the captain ever looked as calm? Is he mad?"

The renowned Captain, nauseous, staring into the tide
Pushed—with struggle—into his own stomach
A thick, veiled splinter of wood

And he bled the darkest red
        As if boundless billows of black spilled
                From a coal-fountain
Into the soundless nightscape,
Onto the barren sand.

So entranced and helpless,
Those of us who watched him die.
That we sat down on the silvered shore
In wait of his coughed reply:

"We are all going to die,"
"We are *all* going to DIE!"

 Part 3
A cypress bent,
   Forlorn,
Above the carmine lake
Floating in the trees of shimmering water

Is every lake forever a falling window
 into the mirror of forever?
They wondered as they fled the shore

A long raft of blood-stained icicles is leaving the ruin of
the camp, ensconced in the fleeting silver fog
A swath of red grasses guiding them across the mirror

Never looking away,
Asleep or possessed of wonder.

The last surviving passenger quivers on his pale, worn
side.

"The Philosophy of Sailing" (excerpt)
by Justin Frederick

Leaving those rendered speechless, and confused. The
tides have turned.
The clouds provide a fortune, that in which, we cannot
read.
The air grows thick, and the fog rolls through the
gloomy hills.
At last, our destiny is drawn but yet, just another inch
closer.
Reflections show our faces without a mask, we are
oblivious.
Like children waiting to find, the ghost inside our head
is not real.
Estranged feelings of isolation, brings comfort for the
evil ones.
They never think to spread their objective. It's what
suits us.

Women in Acrostics

Lost in the Bucolic Vance
Surreal Pastures of Muleshead, Utah,
Scared to be skinned
Or starved in the bogs
"The wild woman of the mountains"
Somewhere with her sisters
Loathe of the quiet walk
From the six-pack in the spring

(For Bukowski)

Seawall of City Lights

Seawall of city lights
A bay of mirrors starred
Only to grow lovelier
As the boat sails away
—Forever from the shore.

Enantiomers and Techgrind Lyrics

Ah, "Laser-Bitch"
Hooded in lambskin
Blackout with me
Beneath the black-light tonight

Here those ragdoll arms
Bend back Aegean-blue
Thin as an electric guitar string—
And pulled far back too soon

With her Robotussin-redolence
  And ghost-like glitter
    The froth of mystery
      Is forever just near

Lo, the Laser-Bitch dances!
Through exotic white charnel houses
Gothic mythopoeic monastery basements
And straight into my heart—

However Does the Ocean Circle the Ion Sphere

I wouldn't change what came;
I held my hands to the sky,
then forged a cloud from the soil,
and, I wept against the riverbank and ruined my clothes

I wrote her a long letter saying
forever I will love you
But there is nothing left for us,
Here and now, if ever there was

However does the sky pull back the horizon
How does the well constrict?
Pressed into the snow,
However do these ashes glow
And has this great mind wept for those before us?

However do we know
When the mushroom clouds fall below
Can we then begin to grow?
Will we finally learn from what we already know?

The Neighbor

It's late fall, in my twenty-third year, and I have rented a cottage by Fall Creek, draped and wreathed so heavily in the iridescent foliage of New York pine that, to the rest of the world, the cottage is essentially lost. I want more than anything to get away from the tumid disquiet of campus life and truly take time to develop my affinity for the pen, with privacy and silence and anonymity, for this next winter.

The cottage is owned by a dapper man of military inheritance who maintains many affairs in other quarters of (and often across) the countryside, away for many months at a time. And so he welcomes a bold, snow-proof lodger by offering amicably low rent while requesting few responsibilities.

The driveway, patched with flagstone and dry-russet sunflowers, is parted several hundred feet beyond the main road, leading to the ambage of another cottage too far away to see, and here lies the onus of his one inexorable rule: DO NOT ENCOUNTER THE NEIGHBOR AT ANY COST. He'd plead to me earnestly the unsavory hostility and pervasive, almost incredulous *hysteria*, of the autumnal woman with whom he shared the only path to his cottage for almost half of his life. For nearly an hour on the day that I received the keys, he raved about contentions and catastrophes and the

32

inveterate injustice of purchasing land adjacent to a loon. I didn't know how to take his screed, or in what light or context. As a legitimate screed of justified repudiation? As a time-honored foul mood? As foolishness on both accounts? Most likely, I thought, something fabricated over decades, so long standing as to continue without bend to resolution. I didn't know what to think, but I could not have cared less since I had no intention of becoming civic-minded or otherwise engage myself in the restless, rural neighborhood community.

The weathered cottage looks ancient and unkempt, yet quaint next to the water. A decorticate millrace runs behind a narrow, toppling shed in which I vow never to go; not so much for fear of the structure collapsing in on me but more of snakes, and cautioned by the modern horror-picture. The great ledge that falls abruptly, allows a line of sight from the roof overlooking the wild, open field. This is what sold me on the arrangement at almost any price. I had to have it, even if I was pledged to extricate myself from any discourteous tidings with some cavewoman shouting bavardage and pointing at me with a stick of driftwood brandished in the wind like a *Sabre of Truth.*

All has been worthwhile since moving in, and after ten peaceful days and nights with no sign of aforesaid neighbor, I feel I am due a reward, complete with a change of scenery.

I secure a reclining lawn chair to my back with a belt, I stuff a bottle of J&B in one coat pocket and a pack of Pall Malls in the other, and I climb up a hardy trellis to the cottage rooftop near the great ledge.

I pick a spot on the flat roof to set up my chair, one that has a clear view of the open field. I dig out the bottle of J&B, take several swigs, then find my cigarettes and light one up. I sit enjoying the crisp November air breezing by in stark contrast to the warmth of the afternoon sun.

Looking across the field and over the polished water, I saw every color the eye has ever conceived since the beginning of time. Acres and acres stretching the scroll of technicolored vine, stretching the green and rust and flavous canvas, stretching my tired heart whenever my eyes wavered beyond the waterline.

I finally notice that I have drank the bottle down to the last few ounces, and have smoked half a pack. I laugh to myself, thinking that I'm way too drunk to be on a roof! And then I begin to wonder if I have it in me to climb back down.

I resolve to just sleep it off on the roof, after all, it is flat and I can't imagine I'd roll far enough to the edge to go straight over. But then, a sudden noise startles me. A machine coughs thrice and then loudly roars. *It's coming from the direction of the Mad Bitch!*

Thoughts in the forefront: it's a grave mistake to exile your every neighbor. What if the cottage catches fire and I need to phone 911? What if I am attacked by a bear and need to phone 911? What if I get drunk and fall off my roof and need to phone 911!?

Then I see her, and it all comes together, making some kind of senile sententious sense to me. *Holy Shit.* Weltering and bouncing up and down like soft porn on the lemon-yellow seat of a grass-green John Deere lawn tractor emerges a woman clad in a pinned together flannel Texas quilt and a football helmet, a shotgun leaning upright to her left.

"Mother of God ... she's wearing driving gloves!" I blurt out, chuckling. I sit back down on the lawn chair, feeling safe to watch as long as I don't move much ... or fall.

Her hair flares from the sides of the helmet, an ardent wire of goldenrod, electrocuted way too many times by Dr. Frankenstein's gimp. Her face remarks 'A Beauty in Youth,' a beauty that's been faded by years and years of isolation and craziness. The lawn looks as if it had been mowed the day before, and it probably had. I sit studying her after the laughter gave out. A faint curlicue of sunlight begins to thin to a few narrow strands, but I can still see her perfectly, frayed plaid quilt catching the wind like a cape sheathing a demented superhero.

Maybe I'm just drunk, but I can no longer take the ridiculousness of the sight. I begin to ponder the life in the scotch, and the ledge of the ravine. I really don't want to have a conversation with her.

I can jump off the roof into the outlet and then crawl in the back door without being seen ... But is it deep enough? It wasn't long ago I messed up my back jumping off a bridge to win over that girl ... Don't be a pussy. Leap, damn you! Leap!

I get up slowly and walk to the edge of the roof, waddling with my bottle like a stoned acrobat. The fall is about thirty feet, and relatively safe as long as I don't clip the ledge. *Why not.* I amble backward and swoop up the bottle, take a three-swallow pull, and bend over shuddering with determined sickness. Suddenly, the roar of the lawn mower engine dies to utter stillness, then the sound of the throttle being adjusted. Either I jump now into the pitch-black water below the ledge, or I get trapped on the roof shouting back and forth with the incredulous spinster. For a split second, I think about the awkward exchange, trying to convince the insufferable woman that I'm not a burglar, and not to shoot me.

And I plunge into the abysm, formless in the sky, and crack the surface of the freezing water.

* * *

Since that afternoon, I haven't seen the neighbor press out from her property line during daylight. But on nice nights, at nine sharp, I can hear the distant hiccups of the tractor's engine and I've glimpsed the darting refractions of headlight from that old John Deere. I've stayed off the roof and use the back door exclusively. An entire winter has passed, and we've never been introduced by any common circumstance. And the craziness has stayed behind the pine row.

June

There was a fierce squall above our lakeside cottage
After which, a light from the glassine red-doom sky
Looked down upon our walls,
And pulled her away,
Rising by her chest into the florid, summer evening.

In the morning,
Her ringtone—an ignoble clarion—
Shallowed the sentiment of my far away dream
It woke us up and it wished us
Another pensive glance
For which there was no beginning
And no one could ever end.

Raspberry Ashes Splashed

Warmed in rain drops
The color of her hair—
And the blush of summer—
Clementine and coral

She made me walk on the other side of the street
When I called her a courtesan
Because I wouldn't tell her what it meant
Just until we reached the park gates
Where raspberry ashes splashed in the yellow aspen
That made her want to forget

She had a large, white dog on a leash
Like a tattered flag in the gusting wind
And when I awkwardly freed him to the pathway
He was stifled by briar and
Limping sideways into a maelstrom.

When we reached the bridge, we parted ways
But I begged for her to stay:
"This life will take you nowhere,
Just like every other story
Like every "sandcastle plan.""

The Amazing Lives We Wait

Pale machines threaten their importance
By falling apart
In cheerless, wintry distances.

You call, gasping at a stranger's door
that will shut in your face …

"But, ma'am, my car has broken down!"
"Sir, don't you know that everyone outside these walls
is a rapist."

And what of nostalgia?
Of the amazing lives we wait for,
Days of long ago
Before our parents began to lock the windows.

Will we *will* to walk again,
—Away from our cupboards
—Away from Glorious television
    (The Wheel Chair of the Mind)
Even if there's nowhere to go?

In a Shed under Water

A relentless witch-woman rants
Promises which are measured by her guilt,
Her hair is a smoking sherry-color,
Illuminated under a bare bulb.

In the alley, a wino finger paints on the white wash
Which is dappled in dust and semen.
A stripper, passing by his dirty claw, circles the
concrete stairwell.

Mad villagers nearby
Put out fires in the trash,
And pull a cat, squawking like an old man,
Into the bushes.

"One day their barren lives
Could possibly contribute precious little
To the rest of the dregs of society,
With sobered smiles of chagrin and blame,"
—One doctor said to another, sardonically.

As I See More Glass (with Amanda Shaw)

A young man lay prone on the golden sand, as I read the story again. I've read this story so many times that once, for an unaccountable moment, our realities were married. The phone was ringing from inside room 507. A young woman answered: "Hello."

I had a short time to find him, propped on his elbows, his severe eyes facing the sun. I had read his story so many times that my feet moved themselves knowingly towards where an agitated Mrs. Carpenter was busy slathering her daughter Sybil with a jar of antiquated bronze. I passed them, and ran obliquely a quarter mile across the soft beach. There certainly *was* time to save him, but it was very short.

"Hello, Sybil," he said, never parting his eyes with the bright horizon.

"Excuse me, sir. I am not Sybil. But are you Mr. Glass?"

"I am," he said, eyes closed.

"You *are* Seymour Glass!?"

"Yes, that's me."

He shifted onto his stomach and fixed his stern eyes to mine.

After a nervous pause I began: "Mr. Glass, *see-more*, I cannot really explain to you who I am or where I am from. I fear I cannot begin to fathom exactly where we are now, but would you mind if we were to speak a short while?"

"What do you mean you can't explain who you are, or where you aren't, or why you were born?" Seymour replied inquisitively, without a hint of alarm.

"I am here to help you, in some kind of way; though I'm not yet sure quite how it will work."

"Well, I have planned to go down to the ocean with my friend, Sybil, but until she arrives I suppose we can carry on awhile," he answered with his eyes still affixed to mine. "But please do try to *explain* yourself," he added with the childish warmth of asking an impossible question.

"Do you know why you're here?" I gasped. "You're stuck Seymour; J.D. has trapped you here." My teeth clenched down hard onto my cuticles.

"Who is J.D. and why is he trying to trap me in my vacation?" he asked, bemused.

"It's Salinger. J.D. Salinger. And this is not your vacation. You are in a story, Seymour, one of nine—and I'm trying to save you."

"Well, are the other eight any good?" Seymour smirked, and then casually added, "What I mean to say is, what else do you know about me?"

I had it on good authority that Seymour enjoys talking. What I needed was to wind him up, and with such little time I needed to get somewhere fast.

"You're here with Muriel, your wife?"

"Yes, she's quite lovely and well taken care of; her family is quite awful," he explained. I stared at him blankly as he carried on:

44

"They're just so nervous, constantly. Her mother calls her, chattering nervously about absolutely nothing. Muriel though is quite lovely. Sometimes she is boring, but lovely still. Her family finds me odd …"

"I know Seymour; she tells them *every*thing about you, doesn't she?"

"Why, yes, I suppose she does; she told them about the scars on my wrist; she told them how I once drove off into the trees." A voluble smile suddenly stretched across his mouth. "And her father is positively loathe of my humor, especially the sort about the dead cats."

I already knew about Muriel, and her family, and their demeanor. I knew his answers, but I needed to hear it from Seymour; so I could wake him up and bring him back to life. At this point I grabbed the manuscript from the shallow pocket of my summer shorts and I began reading to him:

"I said he drove very nicely, mother. Now, please. I asked him to stay close to the white line, and all and he knew what I meant, and he did. He was even trying not to look at the trees—you could tell."

I inflected to him how I thought his Muriel was wont to speak. He shifted around in his robe lightly and asked, "What *are* you reading? That voice sounds strangely familiar. I did drive quite nicely all the way down to Florida this year."

"Where was Seymour when you talked to him?" I declaimed from the story in the voice of an overly concerned maternal parent, *"In the Ocean room, playing the piano. He's played both nights we've been here."*

45

"What *is* that that you're reading again?" he asked, as if he had ignored almost everything I had just read. I sighed, and looked down on the sparkling sand.

"Today, as I have said, I am waiting for Sybil," he exclaimed.

"Yes, I know," I replied. "To bananafish."

At that Seymour's body stiffened. His gaze became hard and rattled. I knew then that I had gotten through to him.

"What do *you* know about bananafish!? You possibly cannot! Let me see that book of yours." His robed arm weakly swiped at the air between us.

"Well, I know they lead a tragic life," I confessed as I shifted the book in my hands. It was finally Seymour's turn to stare as I had.

"Looking like a normal fish, but upon swimming into a banana hole they turn into some sort of banana-bloated beast, having eaten far too many."

"They behave like pigs!" he admitted.

"Right you are; and they become so fat they cannot escape back through the hole—"

"And they get banana fever and they die," finished Seymour sadly.

I grinned at the knowledge that I had reached the exact point where I would change everything. I passed the book to Seymour, who opened it to page sixteen where I had intentionally left the leatherette bookmark.

"How has this been written?" he demanded. "How did you know that they swim in schools of six?"

"I've been trying to tell you; I've read everything there is to know about you, Seymour," I replied shyly.

"J.D. has written it all down, *every*thing, and if you carry out page eighteen you'll be trapped in this time and this place, *ad infinitum*, just like the bananafish. It's horribly sad Seymour. I just want to help you."

We sat together for a while. Seymour had rolled to the sand dappled back of his blue terrycloth robe.

"Dear friend," he said light-heartedly. "I knew you were like everyone else. I guess you do somehow already know that I am a paranoid person in reverse. I fear that everyone is trying to make me happy." Seymour knowingly smirked again, and pulled a sausaged white towel across his eyes. And that smirk seared through me deeply. Just like that it was gone; we both knew what was about to happen, matter not what I had done nor tried. Despite my obviously obsessive investment in saving Seymour's life, it was already written and in order to change such A Perfect Day for Bananafish we would have to rewrite every wonderful word that is the Seymour I've loved for so long.

"I wonder where is old Sybil?" he said at last.

"I'll bet she is off somewhere with Sharon Lipschitz," I laughed.

"How unlikely!" he urged, laughing also at the improbability of my statement.

Suddenly a sunburst of tiny feet pattered across the sand.

"Hey. Hello, Sybil," he said, letting the towel fall away from his eyes.

"Are you going into the water?" garbled her little bundle of energy.

"I was waiting for you. What's new?"

"What?"

"What's new? What's on the program?" He queried mawkishly. And with that he stood up, shed his robe, and began to walk away with young Sybil kicking up sand—kicking up sand together in stride.

"This is *yellow*," I heard Sybil say.

"What a fool I am," replied Seymour.

The story was almost finished, as was Seymour. I watched them reach the water, when I realized Seymour knew all along what was written; because he wrote it. Seymour was too smart for us; Seymour wanted to die.

"Hey, Seymour!" I called. "Don't look at my feet."

"What?"

"Never mind. Goodbye, Seymour."

The Favonian Eclipse

The tattered ghost of Favonius;
Who last kissed the branches frail
With a tell-tale swoon
Ending his love divine
—and his eternity dissolute.

Ivy-towered, in the land of hyperbolean night
Where the shadows float languidly
Reside the fey men of a thousand lives,
Who speak in the ancient tongue,
And are rumored to know that which the gods
themselves cannot imagine;
All the knowledge in the universe,
And every heartless ruin below the secret hells of
Tartarus.

For them, he lifted, just once, their magic fires from the
pyre stones into his palms
Which rapturously blossomed into ethereal blue
hurricanes,
Up into the celestial arch of the sky, and then,
The entire world was awash in the ghostly swirling of
an immense tempest.

No one could speak or move among these men who
have forever lived.

And with this, his last gift,
In a billowy, dying form of frail diamond-blue flashes
Dissolving into the ether
The specter of Favonius left
And returned the storms to the sky.

Pamela Susan, Cloy with Grief

Cloy with grief
And surprise
So it is so, Pamela Susan.
You've come to me
From that restive, festival race,
Returned with Greenwood's charming queries
    —And the poet's soft heart
Dry yourself in the wildflowers
Before you drop away, again, from this place.

The Morning of Pamona and Vertumnus

All the morning I wandered in cheerful reverie
through the gardens
Where gorgeous metallic reeds graced the wooden gates
as they opened
All the day I drank wine below the fronds of the willow
while wresting my wrists into writing of the orchards
        of Pamona and Vertumnus

Somniferum

In the scarlet autumn hours of the daylight-dream
The shadows of mirth pour onto my favorite wall
And the sun enfolds the shimmering trees of smoke
    Dancing and painted in sinopia fresco
    Alive! And laughing!

And when the daylight-dream shatters,
    Try to remember the forest,
    Remember the stream,
    Remember the church stones and whispers
    Remember the fading sun enshrined in cerulean
    twilight.

For Ava

Holiday!
And of course, hooray!
Held for us in somber halls
With seldom cheer
In horrid weather,
Still, and so, we're unimaginably happy!

We can break down to dance
We can scream coy at wandering walls
(Like the impression of you I cherish the most)

The tables are kicked over
And the joy is all around,
Smeared with everything in the universe that's colored
in crayons

And we're all so wrapped in wonder, or bliss
That life ponders,
And wonders why
The asterisk of the bower
Doesn't spell out your name
In crude italics
Ava!
AVA!

I think we'll be friends
In fact, I've seen it…
If crazy old men can sometimes imagine the future
We'll go swimming, and share out dreams at breakfast
And reframe the pictures,
That first cast me and your father.

I'm poor!
And strangled and held still!
But I hope that on your birthday,
Since I can't offer you a real present
You'll remember my words.

Love you kiddo,
--*Kyle*

Everyone in the World

So celebrate all the over-grown yards
And hurricanes,
And hysterical bards
Halloween dances in hill-top manors
The hollowed ravine where our children caught snakes

Carouse beneath the cypress
Where you went off the road
And bray with glittered girls
Who have nowhere else to go

There really is something beautiful
About everyone in the world
And I've fallen in love with all of it
Ever since I first knew.

An Interview with the Author

This mini-tête–à–tête appeared July 28, 2012, on my blog The Education of a Pulp Writer and was meant as a pithy primer to introduce Kyle's name to a broader world. —*David Cranmer*

DC: Who are your primary influences and why?

KJK: I was originally influenced by the life of Jim Morrison when I began writing because he was the first character in my life, or in a book, or in history that I was able to naturally and genuinely identify myself with as a young man. After Morrison grew out of fame and pop culture, he walked around a lot anonymously; in gardens and mazes and throughout some of the most remarkable cities in the world. He was determined to live up to his own identification with the greatest of the poets. I believe he wrote about 1600 poems in his life, and I think eventually a clearer visage of history will deign to adequately respect his achievements in literature. I've thought that the identity of a poet (or of my conception of the life of a poet) was a blessed and noble ideal since I was very young ... and part of that was inspired by Morrison.

It wasn't until I began to read Vladimir Nabokov, and soon after Arthur Rimbaud, that I began to appreciate writing (and literature) "in itself" and devoid of any relationship to the formation of an identity or to a philosophical ideal or something like that. A girlfriend had left Lolita at my house when I was seventeen and I was obsessed with the fey solipsism of the character Humbert Humbert. Not so much for his horrid affinities, of course; but, in order to imitate the genius of Humbert's hand, I had to greatly expand my use of the English language.

I wrote all the time and studied literature feverishly for a couple years after that, and I really learned to love the art of language. Rimbaud's "A Season in Hell" is something that I came across in that time. It's one of the most originally brilliant, eccentric and exciting articles that I have ever read in my entire life. I think I've read all of Paul Schmidt's translations of Rimbaud by now, and I have to assent that I've been irrevocably inspired, and maybe even to an extent complimented by my postured fidelity to Rimbaud's work.

DC: Why write poetry? It is known to be a hard sale, and, with the exception of a few chosen, most poets would go hungry trying to make a living from it.

KJK: I never really thought about that until after I had been writing poetry for many years. When I began writing I was a teenager, and an idealist, and I remember being passionately determined to learn about different ways that I could survive and be happy without living by money. I don't want to make a living as a poet as much as I want to perfect myself as a writer for my own private joys. I like poetry the most as a form of expression because of any of the art forms that I know of, it offers your audience the greatest degree of participation on the part of their own mind. And not just their active consciousness. A great poem can access thoughts and feelings that you may not have been aware you had. Pieces of your life that aren't always current or held together. For example, a poem can return to you dreams that you will never remember but have shaped you forever, once long ago, and you may or may not know why. I think it's fascinating, exciting, and important to provoke and expand your mind, and reading and writing poetry is a fantastic way to do that.

DC: A lot of your poetry touches on nature and your fondness for it. Where does that come from?

KJK: It's very hard for me to reminisce genuine moments of happiness from my life, and the few that

I can afford are from a childhood replete with explorations and adventures in the forests. That and much of my early work was written by the side of a large secluded pond on my parent's property.

DC: What's next on your agenda?

KJK: Well, my plan is to organize a few more volumes of my earlier work and get it out there so that I can focus on the creative element of writing again ... the fun part.

A Friend's Eulogy

Kyle was the most intelligent person I have ever had the honor to call one of my best friends. His wonder and love of knowledge was always inspiring to me. We would sit for hours talking about our hopes and dreams. As long as I had known Kyle, my life was always better with him around. There were rough times also, but he was such a good and caring friend, that I would never stay angry with him. He gave me hope for humanity when he would tell me about what he believed was wrong with our world and how we should change it. I would think, "Wow, someone who really understands and sees the world clearly."

I remember many nights when he would call me and other people just to discuss whatever was on his mind. He made me glad to be alive. We had many journeys, some amazing, others bad, but at the end of them we would at some point get together and discuss why things happened the way they did, to put a better understanding on situations. I loved talking with him about everything and he would always meet me with a big smile. He has brought happiness and sorrow to so many peoples' lives. I am sad that he is gone because we were going to do so much. He loved me and everyone else who would have a conversation with him. Knowing he cared for all of us and we cared for him is one of the most important things we can remember.

When we first started spending afternoons together after school, Kyle tried to teach me how to skateboard. I never got very good at it, but we enjoyed each other's company. Kyle thought he had become too old to skateboard ever again or do many other things he thought he had waited too long to accomplish. I told him, "You're crazy, you're only 23." He always had the mindset of someone who was older than he really was. I think before the end he started to realize he was not old, and could do everything that he wanted to, and would. One day Kyle told me that I must come over, because he had started skateboarding again; trying to convince me to join him, with me saying, "Wait man, I think I am too old for this now."

Kyle also loved music so much. I remember many times sitting with him and our friend Matt, listening to them playing guitar. I was amazed at how they worked together to play songs, sometimes even feeding off each other's excitement and happiness from doing what they love. I am angry and heartbroken because I know he has left us all behind and we all will have to live this life without him, but I am grateful that he was in my life and so many others. I am thankful for this and that I was able to spend time with him. The time I knew Kyle for, was the best part of my life.

Kyle loved his family more than anyone or anything. He would talk about his sister all the time.

Sometimes he would say, "Oh, Kayla's mad at me again," and I would laugh, saying, "Again man, what did you do now?" and he would say, "I don't know." I would then ask, "Are you mad at her?" and he would tell me, "I can't stay mad at her, she's my sister, I love her." Then I would talk to him later and he would say, "We're okay now." They would fight and no matter what, always make up. Something only brothers and sisters who love each other deeply could do.

If Kyle was standing right here, I would like to believe he would be smiling at me, because I wrote this for him, and he always wanted everyone to write. He thought writing was the most important thing any one of us could do. He had such an extensive vocabulary, that he would even shock college professors. No one had a way with words like Kyle and I know if he were here, he would have something poetic and breathtaking to say about his passing. Kyle, we all love you and miss you, and you will always be in our thoughts. Bob, Meta, thank you so much for Kyle, he was more than a friend or a best friend, he was a reason to hope for a brighter future.

—Aaron Warner
June 22, 2013

About the Author

Kyle J. Knapp

(Sep 1, 1989 – Jun 18, 2013) was a poet, musician, and short story writer from Freeville, New York. He enjoyed nature, fishing, and playing guitar. He studied social sciences at Tompkins Cortland Community College and worked for the school as an English tutor. His debut collection of poetry, *Pluvial Gardens*, was released in 2012.

Bonus Story:

TWIN TALK by Patti Abbott

From the short story collection
The Lizard's Ardent Uniform
Vol. I of the Veridical Dreams series,
based on the dream journals of
Kyle J. Knapp.

ABOUT THE VERIDICAL DREAMS SERIES

The Veridical Dreams series began in memory of Kyle J. Knapp, poet and writer who passed away in a house fire in 2013 at the age of twenty-three. His dream journals served as the inspiration for a collection of wide-ranging short stories fleshed out from fragments taken from these sleep-derived mind trips.

TWIN TALK
Patti Abbott

Wendy came home at six, done-in after six hours of unpacking donations at the Center. There was always at least one "ugh" moment—which was why the receiving clerk was advised to wear gloves. Today, badly stained baby clothes had been pitched into a soggy-bottomed carton. Spit-up, pureed peas, and sweet potatoes, Wendy guessed, tossing the whole thing into a recycling bin. She'd be assigned to some other task after tomorrow, thank God. It was an awful job, paying minimum wage, but the only sort of work available after her previous employer, a fine arts book store, closed overnight.

As she hung up her jacket in the foyer, Wendy could see the girls were sitting on the sofa doing that cat's cradle thing again with a skein of maroon yarn. A pointless exercise as far as she could tell, another excuse to entwine themselves in a way that couldn't be called odd—though it was. It was weird when they were eight, weirder still at thirteen.

Tying knots was another recent obsession. They'd come home from a library book sale with an old Boy Scout handbook and learned to tie each of the fancifully named knots. They'd insisted on buying the recommended gauged rope at a marine supply store, so everything was by the book—or shipshape—as the guy behind the counter said. She'd no idea there were so many types of knots and worried that a future as dominatrices awaited the girls. Where did these interests come from?

Unlike other mothers of teenage children, she'd give anything to have them texting friends, listening to questionable music, watching movies on their phones. The girls didn't need electronic devices to communicate with each other; they didn't even have to open their mouths. It was as if an invisible wire went from one head to the other. What did that doctor call it? Idioglossia? But idioglossia used signs and made-up words. The twins used a sort of telepathic communication. Shaking her head, she ignored their cradling—having been told many times that disregarding it was the best way to handle minor behavioral abnormalities.

"Do I draw the line at knives?" she'd asked only last week. "That's the next chapter in the book. The proper care and handling of penknives. I called the B.S.A. and was told there was no official policy on the use of knives. It appears that camp-crafting is dependent on penknives for various tasks. It's strictly a troop decision. I didn't have the guts to tell the guy it was two girls following the manual—not an official troop."

"The Boy Scout organization dates from a different era," her therapist told her. He had that soothing tone in his voice again. "Pioneering skills were practical a century ago. Many of the kids came from rural areas. They often belonged to the 4-H group too."

Did he really think she didn't know all of this? "Next I think they're on to building campfires. Don't you think all this interest in potential weaponry is leading to something?" She could feel a rope tightening around her neck.

"You're allowing your imagination to run away with you. Save your concern for behavior with a violent or misanthropic aspect to it," one doctor or another (she changed doctors frequently) had told her whenever she mentioned the mind games they liked to inflict on her, or the way she was excluded from their inner lives. There was plenty of worrisome stuff to discuss. She flopped down on his or her sofa once every fortnight and spilled her guts for 50 minutes. Her ex-husband paid for it as part of the divorce settlement. He'd put up almost no fuss when the item "therapy for Wendy" appeared on the settlement papers.

"Don't you think it's the girls who need therapy though?" he asked her. But they seemed quite content in the world they'd created. It was she who suffered from insomnia, anxiety, self-pity.

"Hey, girls! No homework tonight?" she asked with a false gaiety, beginning to remove the items she needed from the fridge. She could swear she'd bought baby carrots, but only a bag of limp regular-sized spears greeted her. The girls only ate certain foods and baby carrots were a staple. Like two blurry rabbits, they dashed back and forth to the fridge all day long loading up on them. She could hear them crunching from their bedroom at night, the sound rising as her insomnia took hold.

"It's Friday," they said in unison, laughing at both her forgetfulness and their spontaneous response. Judith's voice, as usual, was a half-note ahead of Lilith's. She was always the leader, and in the rare instances the two were separated, Lilith seemed unsure of what to do—as if her plug had come undone.

"Of course. Silly old me." Now that she worked six days a week, Friday night had lost all of its meaning.

They looked up for a minute, and she felt their otherness flow across the room. It was like something physical—a current perhaps—and she stepped back. Their faces showed little interest in the object of their gaze—their mother. Their respect had disappeared when their father left, swirling down the drain even more quickly when she took the job as an hourly worker at the resale shop. Wendy looked enviously at mother-daughter duos coming into the store to peruse the racks together. Just the other day, she watched a teenager share a text message with her mother. Oh, for such inclusion. Producing two of them insured her future as a useless appendage.

Teary eyed, she watched her blonde-haired daughters merge in a swirl of late afternoon sunlight and dust motes. They especially enjoyed sitting on that sofa, knowing somehow that the mellow light of late afternoon enhanced their beauty, that the soft apricot fabric was especially flattering. The mirror, on the wall across from the sofa, made their number swell to four. Every few minutes, one or both glanced in the mirror, smiling at what they saw. Wendy wondered what it was like to take such pleasure in your image. Oh, how empowering to be confident of just rewards and certain outcomes. Her mother had drummed such assurance out of her long before thirteen, convincing her that she was careless, untidy, thick-headed.

If Bill were still available for household chores, she'd have him take the mirror down and replace it with her grandmother's wedding ring quilt—a piece of work that reflected a hardscrabble life during the Depression, where beauty and warmth were made with your hands, not found in a mirror.

On learning they were expecting twins fourteen years ago, Bill was so taken with the idea that he tracked down a woman out west who made bronze casts of pregnant bellies. The woman advertised her sculptures as "stomachs of copper" that would be a permanent celebration of the months of pregnancy. They'd sent for the material, called a Mama's Belly Casting Kit, and spent an evening laying plaster strips across her belly. The cast pulled away after a while, and then they packed it up and mailed it off, wrapped in the simple pages of newspaper recommended by the sculptor. Six weeks later, the twins already born, it came back, a copper bowl with a gong. It was grotesquely large to her, never having really seen herself full on. It was a miracle her abdomen hadn't split open like a fallen watermelon.

According to the website, each bowl made a different sound. Theirs was quite deep and resounding. She'd been skeptical, but the bowl was lovely despite its almost macabre presence in their house. She never found a proper place for it so it drifted from the dining room table, to the fireplace, to the coffee table. Sometimes she filled it with flowers; other times fruit. At Christmas it was stuffed with pine cones and greens. But mostly it sat empty now, a sad reminder of the hopefulness from that period of her marriage. Occasionally they'd demonstrate the gong, mostly to explain its purpose to a visitor. Whereas once it sounded reassuring, it now made the loneliest sound she could name.

After studying the literature on twins fourteen years ago, Bill and Wendy decided to dress the girls differently and gave them individual, non-gender specific toys, trying to encourage separate identities. As soon as the twins could remove their dissimilar clothes, they did so, running naked through the house until she gave in and bought the identical outfits they craved. They shared a single toy at a time, passing it back and forth, fashioning clothes for the stuffed rabbit or bear or dog they preferred to play with from the clothing they no longer wore.

Strange incidents and interests were commonplace with the girls. They'd come upon a set of jacks, tucked away in a box from Wendy's mother's childhood, and played the game incessantly between the age of eight and ten. They liked games where they could work together, and if the rules didn't offer that option, they altered them. With the game of jacks, one of them tossed the ball and the other scooped the jacks.

"But you're missing the point," she told them. "It's doing both things at once that's the trick. Whoever picks up the most jacks without dropping the ones in his hand wins."

They looked at her like she was speaking Portuguese.

"Oh, Mother," Judith finally said. "Where's the fun in that?"

Starting very early on, both girls refused to answer to their given names: Charlotte and Sophie. By the age of eight, they'd renamed themselves, announcing they were to be called Judith and Lilith.

"How did they come up with those names?" Bill had asked her. "Wasn't Lilith some horrible creature?"

"Lilith was a demon," Wendy said. "And Judith beheaded a man."

"Nice," he said. "You've got yourselves some girls there."

Bill often ignored his role in the procreation of their children. Sometimes she wished she'd beaten him in his flight—wondering what her life might be like without the girls. But mothers can't do such things without becoming a pariah. And he'd have murdered the twins by now, having only the vaguest affection for his daughters.

"Can someone set the table?" she asked now, turning the skimpy chops over in the pan. Chops like these would never have turned up on her table four years ago. She looked up. "Girls?" she said, raising her voice.

In their former home, one that Bill paid for with his large salary as a trial attorney, it might've taken some time to find the twins, and they might not have heard her call. This house, however, was less than 1000 square feet, and they could hear her bellow from any corner. Sullenly they returned to the room, silently setting the table. How much longer would they even pay attention? Could you make a sixteen-year old set a table if she didn't care to? Lilith perhaps. But never Judith.

But then her mood lifted as she remembered that she had a date tomorrow night. Something good had actually happened. And right at the work place she so dreaded. A nice-looking man came in, carrying several boxes of kitchenware.

"I can get a tax receipt for this, right?" he asked, struggling to lower the boxes without the top one slipping off.

She waved the form at him. "You bet. Just fill this out and I'll sign it."

"Do you guys put a value on the stuff? Is that how it works?"

"No. But you can find a list of the amounts you can claim online," she said. "A general idea of what the government allows."

"It's my mother's stuff," he said when he saw her eyeing a robe. "She died a few months ago, and I am just getting her things sorted out."

"Must be an awful job."

In fact, she knew this to be true. Her own mother had died last year. The hardest chore had been deciding what to do with photographs of relatives that no one, including Wendy, could put a name to. Throwing these photos out, disposing of perhaps the last proof of their existence, seemed wrong. In the end, she shredded the pictures of relatives she couldn't name, along with half the ones she could.

Now that the boxes sat on the table, she could see there was no band on his finger. "Are you doing this all by yourself?"

"Looks like it. My brother's doing the financial stuff. Lena—my sister's—filling out various forms. So I probably got off the easiest." He smiled. "But I'm the one with the muscle."

"I can see that," she said.

Somehow they moved on to a time to meet for a drink after work. She panicked over what to tell the girls. In the four years that Bill'd been gone, she'd never been on a date—or even out much at night with friends. So she lied, telling the twins she was meeting a fellow employee for coffee. They seemed supremely uninterested. A few days went by, and then Craig called her, suggesting dinner on Saturday night.

Friday night dinner with the girls was the silent affair it usually was—with her, unsuccessfully, trying to get a conversation going. If the girls talked at dinner, it was with each other. Wendy was only called upon for money, her approval of a school trip, a car ride to some event, help with a task they couldn't complete on their own. They never shared anything important with either parent.

They put the dishes in the dishwasher while she wiped the counters and table. Finally, in desperation, she turned on the kitchen radio. Her go-to station played music from the eighties, a period the girls loathed. She saw them rolling their eyes.

"Do you mind if I change the station," Judith asked. Before she could answer, Judith had found something unpleasantly riotous, driving Wendy from the room.

Just as life seemed about as desperate as it could be, the phone rang.

"Checking in to see what sort of food you like," Craig said, his voice deep and soothing. Since Bill left, her life was composed almost entirely of sopranos and she'd missed the baritone she now heard.

"I like any food that someone else prepares," she said. Did that sound desperate or funny? There was a line between the two that she couldn't find with a map.

"How about Italian? That's usually a safe bet."

They agreed on a time, and she hung up feeling good. She liked the idea that he'd consulted her before making a reservation. Bill never had—just assuming whatever he liked was appealing to everyone. If he ever thought about it at all.

The phone rang again.

"Listen, can the girls come next weekend instead of this one," Bill said, not bothering with any niceties. "Something's come up."

"This is like the third time this month that you've disappointed them."

"Do you really think they give a shit, Wendy?"

"Actually, I have plans."

Not even bothering to ask what, he sighed. "Look, okay, I'll have to pick them up early though. And I might have to go out for a few hours. They can stay alone, right. They do it all the time after school, don't they?"

"Of course. They are thirteen." Another woman, she thought to herself. He went through women like a horny teenager.

"Last time they were here—well look—is thirteen this witchy with other girls?"

For a split second, she considered asking what they did. But when Bill said the very things that she herself thought, it always made her mad. And this was no exception.

"You know, Bill, both girls feel your disapproval—you give off a vibe—even over the phone." There was a lot more she could say, but she stopped there. One of the doctors had told her that if she stopped speaking—just a sentence or two before she felt finished—she'd avoid airing her most hostile and hurtful remarks. It did work when she could bear to do it.

"You can't tell me they aren't weird. We've known that since they were two. Maybe even earlier. Last time they were here, I caught them performing some sort of ceremony with candles out in the garden."

"They just do it to get you going." At least, she hoped that was true. "Look, at thirteen, I wrote poetry about death. Kids stuck anonymous letters in my locker at school. My mother refused to let me shave my legs or wear makeup. I was the last kid I knew to see "Thriller" on MTV. Thirteen's tough." Wendy remembered applying makeup after leaving the house, but those hairy legs were more difficult to deal with.

"Jeez, if I'd known all this twenty years ago we could have saved ourselves a lot of trouble. I might have still married you, but I wouldn't have had kids." He chuckled. "What were the anonymous letters about?"

What were they about? Maybe her hairy legs. "Oh, just kid stuff," she told him. But thinking back on it, more than one note accused her of being a witch. Some of the kids had called her Carrie, in fact. Had she been as strange as her girls? She wished her mother was still alive to ask. Or had she guarded her secrets as closely as the twins guarded theirs? Her mother had not been the type of woman a teenager confided in. Was she?

"And as for your hairy legs. They kept me warm on winter nights more than once."

Like a heat-seeking weapon, he never shied from the kill. "You did call for a favor, right?"

"Yeah, I'll pick them up right after gymnastics. Still into that, right?"

"It's practically the only time they leave the house."

Both girls were extremely agile so gymnastics made sense. She would've preferred them to take up a team sport—like softball or soccer, but gymnastics was better than nothing. They didn't really care for the competitions though and often claimed to be sick in order to avoid them. Their coach chided her for not pushing them harder.

"They could win trophies at a lot of these meets," he told her. "Boost the program and their team mates."

Wendy didn't care that they didn't care. She was happy to get them out of the house for a few hours three or four times a week. Both girls excelled in the floor exercises and the vault. They'd worked up a joint floor performance, which was strictly illegal according to the International Federation of Gymnastics.

"They allow synchronized swimming in competitions, don't they," Judith said. "I don't see the difference."

"Maybe we should try swimming," Lilith said.

Wendy was about tell them about her high school swim team triumphs when Judith interrupted. "Do you really want green hair, Lil? Or those gargantuan shoulders?"

Lilith looked at her feet as she often did after offering an unsolicited opinion.

After working at the resale shop until noon on Saturday, Wendy dropped the girls off at the gymnastics center, overnight bags in tow, and began a leisurely preparation for her date. It'd been ages since she took a bath instead of a hurried shower. And even longer since she manicured and polished her nails, both hands and feet. She knew in her heart such elaborate preparation spelled letdown, but dolling herself up felt good even if the date detonated. Craig seemed like a decent guy, but she'd heard too many tales from friends on the hunt to not look at the dating scene skeptically.

Craig had already told her he divorced in his late twenties. The woman had married him on the rebound from a soured college romance and then rebounded again. He had no children but adored his nieces and nephews and hoped to have some of his own. He was five years younger than Wendy and never finished college, taking his computer skills to a tech position at a community college.

"I'm taking a course here or there," he told her, embarrassed. "I'd like to design software eventually."

"A lot of good my degree in anthropology did me," Wendy assured him. "I should be back in school myself, getting a skill that's more saleable."

They both shrugged off the other's failures and ordered: Wendy, veal piccata; Craig, the lobster ravioli. Conversation came easily, and she took that as a good sign and invited him back. She couldn't help but take advantage of the rare evening that the girls were not at home.

"Another glass of wine or some coffee?" she asked, pulling out a box of cookies she'd bought on the off-chance things went well.

"Decaf?"

She nodded.

Later she'd remember pouring the coffee and setting three shortbread and three peanut butter cookies on a plate. Craig stood behind her, saying something about the blue of the Delftware plates that hung on the kitchen wall.

"Is that a dinosaur? The one in the middle?"

She swallowed a laugh—about to tell him that the animal on the dish was an elephant—perhaps painted by someone who'd never seen one—when a veil of gray descended. Cotton balls stuffed her ears. This was the way it seemed to her at least. Her legs went numb, her fingers tingled, and that was it.

* * *

Wendy awoke to the resounding sound of a gong. Perhaps a minute has passed. Perhaps hours. She looked around, and the first thing she saw was Lilith, gong still in her hand and the bowl, dusty, but gorgeous at her feet. Where had they found it?

"She's awake," Lilith shouted. "Mother's awake. How do you feel, Mother? No, don't try to sit up yet." She rushed toward her fallen mother, dropping the gong with a clatter.

"Give her a second," Judith commanded from the other side of the room. "Let her breathe."

As Wendy turned her head, she saw something else: a sight that took her breath away. A man's body was sprawled on the floor, tied at every conceivable juncture with a dozen short ropes. A gag was stuffed in his mouth. Duct tape covered his eyes. Her fear that he was dead ended when he shook his head violently.

Her tongue was too thick to talk.

"What is it, Mother? She's trying to speak, Judith."

"Just listen a minute, Mother. We found this slimy guy kneeling over you when we walked in," Judith said. "You were passed out on the sofa. He probably gave you Rohypnol."

"What?" Wendy had found her voice. "Gave me what?"

"It's a date rape drug. We learned about it in Sex Ed."

Wendy considered this idea. Was this something a grown man did? She'd been about to have sex with him anyway. Surely he could sense that. Although perhaps he liked his sexual partners inert. She'd heard of such things."

86

"Take the duct tape off, girls. Remove that gag."

"He's only going to deny it," Judith said, not moving. "Let's keep him quiet for a second while we think of our next move."

"Lil, take it off."

Her daughter raced across the room, removing it in one swift movement.

Craig screamed for a second or two, trying to push his shoulder up to his mouth for succor.

"Did you slip me a Mickey, Craig?" Wendy asked, not wanting to wrestle with the name of the drug the girls used. She still felt too weak to rise and instead glared at him from her half-collapsed state. "Is that what happened here?"

"God, no," he said after a few seconds. He looked at Wendy. "Are you kidding? What am I—sixteen?" he paused. He turned his head to the girls, standing together in solidarity. "And I'm thinking of filing charges, you two hellions. Your Mom may have been out cold, but I heard enough of your conversation to figure out what went on here."

"We came in, and you were wrestling with Mother on the couch," Judith said piously. "Probably getting ready to rape her."

"You gotta be kidding," he said and turned to Wendy. "They had those ropes all ready. I saw them drag a bag of snakes—I mean ropes—out of their bedroom. They planned this whole thing."

"You were practically on top of her." Judith looked to Lilith for confirmation and received a curt nod. "Deny it!"

"That's true. I was trying to get her to come 'round. I thought maybe it was food poisoning or some sort of female problem." He looked back to Wendy. "My Mom fainted now and then around menopause."

This was the unkindest cut of all. "I am not *around menopause.*"

She detected a blush beneath the ropes. "Well, I guarantee that if a drug was administered it was not by my hand."

"Maybe it was something in the food," Wendy said. "Some sort of allergic reaction. Why don't you untie him, girls, and let him go. How did this happen anyway? Did you wrestle him to the floor?'

She was beginning to have a sense of pride in the girls. Not many thirteen year olds could dispatch a grown man this handily. And surely their actions spoke of some sort of feeling for her. Did they have the ropes ready? If so, they must have sensed her vulnerability and were ready to step in. But being ready to defend their mother and manipulating the situation were two different things.

"They hit me over the head with that damned gong. At least I have a memory of a similar sound. When I came to I was wrapped like a mummy." A twitter from the girls was squashed by Wendy's glare. He put his hand on his head. "A lump, yes."

"I guess there was some sort of misunderstanding here, Craig. Maybe you should just go."

"I'd certainly like to." He wriggled to demonstrate his position.

"Mother," the girls said in unison. "You're going to just let him get away with it."

"You were positively comatose when we came in." Judith's voice was calm, assured.

"Why are you here anyway, girls?" she asked. "What happened at your Dad's?"

The twins looked at each other. "We had bad vibes," Lilith said. "So once he went out, we came right over."

"We took a taxi even. To get here quickly. We both felt something was wrong and we turned out to be right. He was all over you, Mother. Had a hand down your blouse. Your skirt was up around your waist."

"I was unbuttoning your top button to see if that helped," Craig said. "I was seconds away from an emergency call. Look girls, grown men don't use drugs like that one. What woman wouldn't report him afterward?"

"If she even woke up," Judith said. "If your heinous plot didn't include her death."

Although it was unclear whether or not Judith was correct, Wendy couldn't help a grin.

"I think if Craig had given me a serious drug—like—"

"Rohypnol," her three companions said together.

"Right. Well, if he had, I doubt I would feel right as rain already. So let's unloosen him, please."

Making the same face, the two girls began their task.

89

"It might go quicker with a knife," Lilith said, hopefully.

"No," both Craig and Wendy said together. Within a few minutes, Craig was gone, shaking his head and muttering something about crazy women. Something about witches or perhaps, bitches.

Wendy knew she should be angry and deliver them the lecture of a lifetime. But all she could concentrate on was that her girls had saved her from what they thought was a threat. Now the three of them would be as close as the mothers and daughters she admired in the shop. The ones at the mall, the ones at the movie theater, chuckling over a rom-com.

"So they'll be no more of that, right Mother?"

"What?" she asked coming out of her reverie. Both girls stood in front of her, their eyes hard. "No more of what?"

"No more picking up strange men and bringing them into our home." Judith's voice was as stern as hers might have been if she'd chastised them properly.

"I hardly picked him ..."

"The next time we may not get here in time," Lilith said. "We can't always be on guard."

"Or we may not want to," Judith said. "We only have so much ... patience."

In a minute, the girls had gone off together, shutting their bedroom door firmly. She heard the crunch of carrots, the sound of a shared giggle. She was alone again—any idea of a change in the climate, squashed.

In the mirror across from the apricot sofa, she barely seemed to exist at all. It seemed like those two blonde heads were imprinted on it somehow—a permanent discolor. Perhaps she was slowly disappearing as their image achieved dominance. She'd look for that wedding ring quilt tomorrow—before it was too late.

†

MORE FROM THE VERIDICAL DREAMS SERIES

THE LIZARD'S ARDENT UNIFORM & Other Stories (Vol. I) — Go on a voyage into everyday nightmares, bizarre detours, and hellish worlds through seven stirring tales of crime, mystery, science fiction, fantasy, and literary fiction, inspired from thought-provoking fragments extracted from the dream journals of Kyle J. Knapp. Stories by Chris F. Holm, Terrie Farley Moran, Patti Abbott, Evan V. Corder, Steve Weddle, Hilary Davidson, and Garnett Elliott.

TREASURE OF ICE AND FIRE (Vol. II) by Wayne D, Dundee — A rogue priest, leading a rag-tag band, goes in search for the hammer of the gods, possessing a mystical power that can either free his people, or, in the wrong hands, spell annihilation for mankind. But will he and his crew be the first to reach the hammer and unharness its awe-inspiring magic?

MAGE, MAZE, DEMON (Vol. III) by Charles Allen Gramlich — A barbarian is promised his freedom from a labyrinth of treacherous caverns if he can succeed in retrieving a talisman that will stop a demon of unfathomable power. But first he must survive a sorcerer's maze rigged with flooded tunnels, poisoned traps, and a monstrous beast that can heal its own wounds.

www.beattoapulp.com

42094569R00067

Made in the USA
Middletown, DE
02 April 2017